Cement Hands

by Thornton Wilder

A Samuel French Acting Edition

SAMUEL FRENCH
FOUNDED 1830

SAMUELFRENCH.COM
SAMUELFRENCH-LONDON.CO.UK

Copyright © 1997 by The Wilder Family LLC
Foreword copyright © 2014 by Tappan Wilder
All Rights Reserved

CEMENT HANDS is fully protected under the copyright laws of the United States of America and all countries with which the United States has reciprocal copyright relations, whether through bilateral or multi-lateral treaties or otherwise, and including but not limited to, all countries covered by the Pan-American Copyright Convention, the Universal Copyright Convention, and the Berne Convention. All rights, including professional and amateur stage productions, recitation, lecturing, public reading, motion picture, radio broadcasting, television and the rights of translation into foreign languages are strictly reserved.

ISBN 978-0-573-70388-1

www.SamuelFrench.com
www.SamuelFrench-London.co.uk

For Production Enquiries

United States and Canada
Info@SamuelFrench.com
1-866-598-8449

Amateur Rights in the United Kingdom
Plays@SamuelFrench-London.co.uk
020-7255-4302

Each title is subject to availability from Samuel French, depending upon country of performance. Please be aware that *CEMENT HANDS* may not be licensed by Samuel French in your territory. Producers should contact the nearest Samuel French office or licensing partner to verify availability.

For all enquiries regarding Professional productions in the United Kingdom; Professional and Amateur productions throughout the rest of Europe; and motion picture, television, and other media rights, please contact Alan Brodie Representation (Victoria@AlanBrodie.com). Visit www.thorntonwilder.com/contact for details.

CAUTION: Professional and amateur producers are hereby warned that *CEMENT HANDS* is subject to a licensing fee. Publication of this play does not imply availability for performance. Professionals and Amateurs considering a production are strongly advised to apply for a license before starting rehearsals, advertising, or booking a theatre. A licensing fee must be paid whether the title is presented for charity or gain and whether or not admission is charged.

No one shall make any changes in this title for the purpose of production. No part of this book may be reproduced, stored in a retrieval system, or transmitted in any form, by any means, now known or yet to be invented, including mechanical, electronic, photocopying, recording, videotaping, or otherwise, without the prior written permission of the publisher. No one shall upload this title, or part of this title, to any social media websites.

MUSIC USE NOTE

Licensees are solely responsible for obtaining formal written permission from copyright owners to use copyrighted music in the performance of this play and are strongly cautioned to do so. If no such permission is obtained by the licensee, then the licensee must use only original music that the licensee owns and controls. Licensees are solely responsible and liable for all music clearances and shall indemnify the copyright owners of the play and their licensing agent, Samuel French, against any costs, expenses, losses and liabilities arising from the use of music by licensees. Please contact the appropriate music licensing authority in your territory for the rights to any incidental music.

IMPORTANT BILLING AND CREDIT REQUIREMENTS

All producers of *CEMENT HANDS* must give credit to the author of the play in all programs distributed in connection with performances of the play, and in all instances in which the title of the play appears for the purposes of advertising, publicizing or otherwise exploiting the play and/or a production. The name of the author must appear on a separate line on which no other name appears, immediately following the title and must appear in size of type not less than fifty percent of the size of the title type.

This play may be performed only in its entirety. No permission can be granted for cuttings, readings or any use of parts of the play for any purpose whatsoever without the express written permission of the Wilder Family LLC. Absolutely *no* changes can be made to the text.

FOREWORD TO WILDER'S *CEMENT HANDS*

THE SIN OF AVARICE

From the time he began dreaming up plays as a boy Thornton Wilder's vision of the theater transcended conventional boundaries, and to the end of his life his vision continually evolved and expanded. In 1956, he began work on what grew into an extravagantly ambitious project: two cycles of seven one-act plays based on the Deadly Sins and the Ages of Man. *Cement Hands* represents "Avarice" in Wilder's projected cycle on the Seven Deadly Sins.

In what would prove to be his final dramatic works, Wilder sought not only to explore the theatrical possibilities inherent in the Sins and Ages, but (as he phrased it in his private journal on Christmas Day 1960) to "offer each play in the series as representing, also, a different mode of playwriting: Grand Guignol, Chekhov, Noh play, etc., etc." In short, he envisioned nothing less than a tour de force of dramatic theme and form encapsulated in the economy and intensity of the one-act play.

Wilder did not complete the challenge he set for himself, but he came close. The surviving work enriches his dramatic legacy and deserves to be remembered as more than a footnote to his lifelong conviction (written soon after *Our Town* opened on Broadway in 1938): "The theater offers to imaginative narration its highest possibilities."

THE SINS AND AGES THEN AND NOW

A brief overview of the history of these plays will help readers place them in Wilder's career as a dramatist. Two Sins, *Bernice* (Pride) and *The Wreck on the 5:25* (Sloth), premiered in English at a special event in Berlin in 1957 (with Wilder performing in *Bernice*). For reasons that have never been clear, for he enjoyed the experience and felt that plays did well, he withdrew them. That same year a third Sin, *The Drunken Sisters* (Gluttony), written as the satyr play for Wilder's full length drama, *The Alcestiad*, proved successful in its premiere on the stage of Zürich's fabled Schauspielhaus.

Five years passed before the continuation of his ambitious scheme appeared on a stage in the United States. In January 1962, two new Ages (*Infancy* and *Childhood*) and a new Sin, *Someone From Assisi* (Lust), opened at Circle in the Square, then located off-Broadway on Bleecker Street, to the reported largest pre-opening advanced sale in that stage's then 11- year history. Billed as "Plays for Bleecker Street," the show of ran for 349 performances.

Then silence. After "Plays for Bleecker Street" closed, no more Sins or Ages appeared. When Thornton Wilder died in 1975 the public record of his 14-play scheme contained only four plays – two Ages (*Infancy* and *Childhood*) and two Sins (Lust and Gluttony).

Today, eleven of Wilder's Sins and Ages are available for production: a completed cycle of the seven Deadly Sins and four of seven Ages of Man. The source of the seven "new" plays is no secret. The missing pieces were found in Thornton Wilder's archives at Yale[1]. From this source, starting in 1995, his literary executor and family released the two plays withdrawn in 1957, *Cement Hands* (Avarice), and four additional titles (*Youth, The Rivers Under the Earth* [Middle Age][2], *A Ringing of Doorbells* [Envy] and *In Shakespeare and the Bible* [Wrath]) recovered and completed by the actor, director and friend of Wilder's, F.J. O'Neil. (Mr. O'Neil's valuable notes on the origin of each of these missing links follow the text of each play.)

The public reception of Thornton Wilder's long lost and new plays was gratifying. *The Wreck on the 5:25* was selected as one of the Best American Short Plays of 1994-95. In 1997, the Centenary of the playwright's birth, Kevin Kline starred in a premiere reading in New York of *Cement Hands*, and the works recovered by Mr. O'Neil served as the centerpieces of Actors Theatre of Louisville's 13th Annual Brown-Forman Classics in Context Festival.   Finally, as the capstone to the Centenary celebration, TCG Press in 1997 published the 11 Sins and Ages in Volume I of *The Collected Short Plays of Thornton Wilder.*

---

[1] No additional one-acts remain to be discovered in Thornton Wilder's archives at Yale.

[2] We believe Wilder intended *The Rivers Under the Earth* to represent Middle Age.

Wilder never followed conventional theatrical practice. As a young writer in his "Classic One Act Plays" of 1931, he swept away scenery and played provocative games with time and place. In the Sins and Ages, his farewell as a playwright, he is no less adventurous by way of settings, techniques, stage-craft and themes. One artistic trend of the day especially "fired his imagination" where these plays are concerned: his passionate belief in the value of the arena stage. "The boxed set play," he wrote in 1961, "encourages the anecdote…The unencumbered stage encourages the truth in everyone." Wilder felt so strongly that audiences should be seated as close to the actors as possible that Samuel French, for several years, was only permitted to license these plays to companies agreeing to perform them on a three-sided thrust or arena stage.

***

As part of its celebration of Wilder's one-act plays, Samuel French and the Wilder family take great pleasure in issuing new acting editions for the Sins and Ages long in print and, for the first time, acting editions of the seven new Wilder works. We invite those performing or teaching these plays to visit www.thorntonwilder.com for additional information.

– *Tappan Wilder*,
Literary Executor for Thornton Wilder

CHARACTERS

EDWARD BLAKE, a lawyer, fifty
PAUL, a waiter, fifty-five
DIANA COLVIN, Blake's niece, twenty-one
ROGER OSTERMAN, Diana's fiancé, twenty-seven

SETTING

Corner in the public rooms of a distinguished New York hotel.

(A screen has been placed at the back [that is, at the actors' entrance] to shut this corner off from the hotel guests. A table in the center of the stage with a large RESERVED sign on it. Various chairs. At the end of the stage farthest from the entrance is a low bench; above it we are to assume some large windows looking onto Fifth Avenue. Enter **EDWARD BLAKE**, *a lawyer, fifty. He is followed by* **PAUL**, *a waiter, fifty-five.)*

BLAKE. *(rubbing his hands)* Paul, we have work to do.

PAUL. Yes, Mr. Blake.

BLAKE. There will be three for tea. I arranged with Mr. Gruber that this corner would be screened off for us; and I specially asked that you would wait on us. As I say, we have some work to do. *(smilingly giving him an envelope)* There's a hundred dollars, Paul, for whatever strain you may be put to.

PAUL. Thank you, sir. – Did you say "strain," Mr. Blake?

BLAKE. I'm going to ask you to do some rather strange things. Are you a good actor, Paul?

PAUL. Well – I often tell the young waiters that our work is pretty much an actor's job.

BLAKE. I'm sure you're a very good one. Now the guests today are my niece, Diana Colvin. – You know Miss Colvin, don't you?

PAUL. *(with pleasure)* Oh, yes, Mr. Blake. Everyone knows Miss Colvin.

BLAKE. And her fiancé – that's a secret still – Mr. Osterman?

PAUL. Which Mr. Osterman, sir?

BLAKE. Roger – Roger Osterman. You know him?

PAUL. Oh, yes, sir.

BLAKE. Now it's not clear which of us is host. But it's clear to *me* which of us is host. Roger Osterman has invited us to tea. He will pay the bill.

PAUL. Yes, sir.

BLAKE. There may be some difficulty about it – some distress; some squirming; some maneuvering – protesting. But he will pay the bill.

(*a slight pause while he looks hard and quizzically at* **PAUL**, *who returns his gaze with knowing raised eyebrows*)

Now at about 5:20 you're going to bring Mr. Osterman a registered letter. The messenger will be waiting in the hall for Mr. Osterman's signature. Roger Osterman will ask to borrow half a dollar of me. I won't have half a dollar. He will then turn and ask to borrow half a dollar of you. And you won't hear him.

PAUL. I beg your pardon, sir?

BLAKE. He'll ask to borrow half a dollar of you, but you won't hear him. You'll be sneezing or something. Your face will be buried in your handkerchief. Have you a cold, Paul?

PAUL. No, sir. We're not allowed to serve when we have colds.

BLAKE. Well, you're growing deaf. It's too bad. But…you…*won't…hear* him.

PAUL. (*worriedly*) Yes, sir.

BLAKE. You'll say, (*raising his voice*) "Yes, Mr. Osterman, I'll get some hot tea, at once." This appeal to you for money may happen several times.

PAUL. (*abashed*) Very well, Mr. Blake, if you wish it.

BLAKE. Now, Paul, I'm telling you why I'm doing this. You're an intelligent man and an old friend. My niece is going to marry Roger Osterman. I'm delighted that my niece is going to marry him. He's a very nice fellow and what else is there about him, Paul?

PAUL. Why, sir – it is understood that he is very rich.

BLAKE. Exactly. But the Ostermans are not only fine people and very rich people – they have oddities about them, too, haven't they? – A certain oddity?

(**BLAKE** *slowly executes the following pantomime: he puts his hands into his trouser pockets and brings them out, open, empty and "frozen".*)

PAUL. *(reluctantly)* I know what you mean, sir.

BLAKE. Have you a daughter, Paul, or a niece?

PAUL. Yes, sir. I have two daughters and three nieces.

BLAKE. Then you know: we older men have a responsibility to these girls. I have to show my niece what her fiancé is like. I have to show her this odd thing – this one little unfortunate thing about the Ostermans.

PAUL. I see, Mr. Blake.

BLAKE. I'm not only her uncle; I'm her guardian; and her lawyer. I'm all she's got. And I must show her – here she comes now – and for that I need your help.

(*Enter* **DIANA COLVIN**, *twenty-one, in furs. The finest girl in the world.*)

DIANA. Here you are, Uncle Edward. – Good afternoon, Paul.

PAUL. Good afternoon, Miss Colvin.

BLAKE. Will you wait for tea, Diana?

DIANA. *(crossing the stage to the bench)* Yes.

(**PAUL** *goes out.*)

BLAKE. Aren't you going to kiss me?

DIANA. No!! I'm furious at you. I'm so furious I could cry. You've humiliated me. I'm so ashamed I don't know what to do. Uncle Edward, how could you do such a thing?

BLAKE. *(calmly)* What, dear?

DIANA. I've just heard that –

(She rises and strides about, groping for a handkerchief in her bag.)

– you're asking the Osterman family how much allowance Roger will give me when we're married. And you're making some sort of difficulty about it. Uncle Edward! The twentieth century! And as though I were some poor little goose-girl he'd discovered in the country. Oh, I could die. I swear to you, I could die.

BLAKE. *(still calmly)* Sit down, Diana.

(Silence. She walks about, dabs her eyes and finally sits down.)

Diana, I'm not an idiot. I don't do things like this by whim and fancy.

DIANA. Perfectly absurd. Why, all those silly society columnists keep telling their readers every morning that I'm one of the richest girls in the country. Is it true?

(He shrugs.)

I'll never need a cent of the Ostermans' money. I'll never take a cent, not a cent.

BLAKE. What?

DIANA. I won't have to.

BLAKE. What kind of marriage is that?

(He rises. She looks at him a little intimidated.)

Well, you'll be making an enormous mistake and it will cost you a lot of suffering.

DIANA. What do you mean?

BLAKE. Marriage is a wonderful thing, Diana. But it's relatively new. Twelve, maybe fifteen thousand years old. It brings with it some ancient precivilization elements. Hence, difficult to manage. It's still trying to understand itself.

DIANA. *(shifting in her seat, groaning)* Really, Uncle Edward!

BLAKE. It hangs on a delicate balance between things of earth and things of heaven.

DIANA. Oh, Lord, how long?

BLAKE. Until a hundred years ago a wife *had* no money of her own. All of it, if she had any, became her husband's. Think that over a minute. Billions and billions of marriages where the wife had not one cent that she didn't have to *ask* for. You see: it's important to us men, us males, us husbands that we supply material things to our wives. I'm sorry to say it but we like to think that we own you. First we dazzle you with our strength, then we hit you over the head and drag you into our cave. We buy you. We dress you. We feed you. We put jewels on you. We take you to the opera. I warn you now – most seriously – don't you start thinking that you want to be independent of your husband as a provider. You may be as rich as all hell, Diana, but you've got to give Roger the impression every day that you thank him – thank him humbly, that you aren't in the gutter.

DIANA. *(short pause; curtly)* I don't believe you.

BLAKE. Especially Roger. *(leaning forward; emphatic whisper)* You are marrying into a very strange tribe.

(They gaze into one another's eyes.)

Roger is the finest young man in the world. I'm very happy that you're going to marry him. I think that you will long be happy – but you'll only be happy if you know beforehand exactly what you're getting into.

DIANA. What *are* you talking about?

(She rises and crosses the stage.)

I want some tea.

BLAKE. No, we don't have tea until he comes. *He* is giving us tea. Please sit down. What am I talking about? Diana, you've been out with Roger to lunch and dinner many times, haven't you? You've gotten in and out of taxis with him. You've arrived at railroad stations and had porters carry your bags, haven't you?

DIANA. Yes.

BLAKE. Have you ever noticed anything odd about his behavior in such cases?

DIANA. What do you mean?

(He gazes levelly into her eyes. She begins to blush slightly. Silence.)

BLAKE. Then you have?

DIANA. *(uncandidly)* What do you mean?

BLAKE. Say it!

(pause)

DIANA. *(suddenly)* I love him.

BLAKE. I know. But say what's on your mind.

DIANA. It's a little fault.

BLAKE. How little?

DIANA. I can gradually correct him of it.

BLAKE. That's what his mother thought when she married his father...After you leave a restaurant do you go back and leave a dollar or two for the waiter, when Roger's not looking? Do you hear taxi drivers shouting indecencies after him as he walks away? Have you seen him waste time and energy to avoid a very small expenditure?

DIANA. *(rising, with her handbag and gloves, as though about to leave)* I don't want to talk about this any more. It's tiresome; and more than that it's in bad taste. Who was it but *you* who taught me never to talk about money, never to mention money. And now we're talking about money in the grubbiest way of all – about *tipping*. And you've been talking to the Osterman family about an allowance for me. I feel soiled. I'm going for a walk. I'll come back in twenty minutes.

BLAKE. Good. That's the way you should feel. But there's one more thing you ought to know. Paul will help us.

*(He goes to the entrance at the back, apparently catches **PAUL**'s eye, and returns.)*

DIANA. You're not going to drag Paul into this?

BLAKE. Who better? – Now if *you* sit at ease, it will put *him* at ease.

(*Enter* **PAUL.**)

PAUL. Were you ready to order tea, Mr. Blake?

BLAKE. No, we're waiting for Mr. Osterman. You haven't seen him, have you?

PAUL. No, I haven't.

BLAKE. Paul, I was talking with Miss Colvin about that little matter you and I were discussing. You gave me permission to ask you a few questions about the professional life in the hotel here.

PAUL. If I can be of any help, sir.

BLAKE. The whole staff of waiters is accustomed to a certain lack of…generosity on the part of the Osterman family. Is that true?

PAUL. (*deprecatingly*) It doesn't matter, Mr. Blake. We know that they give such large sums to the public in general…

BLAKE. Is this true of any other families?

PAUL. Well…uh…there's the Wilbrahams.

(**BLAKE** *nods.*)

And the Farringtons. That is, Mr. Wentworth and Mr. Conrad Farrington. With Mr. Ludovic Farrington it's the other way 'round.

BLAKE. Oh, so every now and then these families produce a regular spendthrift?

PAUL. Yes, sir.

BLAKE. I see. Now, have the waiters a sort of nickname for these less generous types?

PAUL. (*reluctantly*) Oh…the younger waiters…I wouldn't like to repeat it.

BLAKE. You know how serious I am about this. I wish you would, Paul.

PAUL. Well…they call them "cement hands."

DIANA. (*appalled*) WHAT?

BLAKE. *(clearly)* Cement hands. – What you mean is that they can give away thousands and millions but they cannot put their fingers into their pockets for…a quarter or a dime? And, Paul, is it true that in many cases the wives of the Ostermans and Wilbrahams and Farringtons return to the table after a dinner or supper and leave a little something – to correct the injustice?

PAUL. Yes, Mr. Blake. – Mrs.…but I won't mention any names…sometimes sends me something in an envelope the next day.

BLAKE. Yes.

PAUL. Perhaps I should tell you a detail. In these last years, the gentlemen merely *sign* the waiter's check. And they add a present for the waiters in writing.

BLAKE. *That* they can do. Well?

PAUL. Pretty well. What they cannot do –

BLAKE. – is to put their hands in their pockets. Thank you. And have you noticed that one of these hosts…as the moment approaches to…

(He puts his hands gropingly in his pockets.)

…he becomes uncomfortable in his chair…his forehead gets moist?…

PAUL. Yes, sir.

BLAKE. He is unable to continue conversation with his friends? Some of them even start to quarrel with you?

PAUL. I'm sorry to say so.

BLAKE. *(shakes* **PAUL***'s hand)* Thank you for helping me, Paul.

PAUL. Thank you, sir.

*(***PAUL** *goes out.* **DIANA** *sits crushed, her eyes on the ground. Then she speaks earnestly.)*

DIANA. Why is it, Uncle Edward? Explain it to me! How can such a wonderful and generous young man be so mean in little things?

BLAKE. Your future mother-in-law was my wife's best friend. Katherine Osterman has given her husband four children. She runs two big houses – a staff of twenty at least. Yet every expenditure she makes is on account it goes through her husband's office – sign for everything – write checks for everything. You would not believe the extent to which she has no money of her own – in her own hand. Her husband adores her. He can't be absent from her for a day. He would give her hundreds of thousands in her hands but she *must ask for it*. He wants that picture that everything comes from him. Why, she has to go to the most childish subterfuges to get a little cash – she buys dresses and returns them, so as to have a hundred dollars in bills. She doesn't want to do anything underhand, but she wants to do something personal – small and friendly and personal. She can give a million to blind children, but she can't give a hundred to her maid's daughter.

(**DIANA**, *weeping, blows her nose.*)

Now you say you have your own money. Yes, but I want to be sure that you have an allowance *from Roger* that you don't have to account to him for. Money to be human with – not as housekeeper or as a beautifully dressed Osterman or as an important philanthropist but as an imaginative human being; and I want that money to come from your husband. It will puzzle him and bewilder him and distress him. But maybe he will come to understand the principle of the thing.

DIANA. *(miserably)* How do you explain it, Uncle Edward?

BLAKE. I don't know. I want you to study it right here today. Is it a sickness?

DIANA. *(shocked)* Uncle Edward!

BLAKE. Is it a defect in character?

DIANA. Roger has no faults.

BLAKE. Whatever it is, it's deep – deep in the irrational. For Roger it's as hard to part with twenty-five cents as it is for some people to climb to the top of a skyscraper, or to eat frogs, or to be shut up with a cat. Whatever it is – it proceeds from a *fear*, and whatever it is, it represents an incorrect relation to –

DIANA. To what?

BLAKE. *(groping)* To…

(PAUL appears at the entrance.)

PAUL. Mr. Osterman has just come into the hall, Mr. Blake.

BLAKE. Thank you, Paul.

(PAUL goes out.)

DIANA. Incorrect relation to what?

BLAKE. To material things – and to circumstance, to life – to everything.

(Enter ROGER OSTERMAN, twenty-seven, in a rush. The finest young fellow in the world.)

ROGER. Diana! Joy and angel of my life.

(He kisses her.)

Uncle Edward. – Ten minutes past five. I've got to make a phone call. To Mother. I'll be back in a minute. Mother and I are setting up a fund. I'll tell you all about it. Uncle Edward, what are you feeding us?

BLAKE. We haven't ordered yet. We were waiting for our host.

ROGER. *(all this quickly)* Am I your host? Very well. You've forgotten that you invited us to tea. Didn't he, Diana?

BLAKE. You distinctly said –

ROGER. *You* distinctly said – really, Diana, we can't let him run away from his responsibilities like that. Uncle Edward, we accept with pleasure your kind invitation –

BLAKE. You called me and told me to convey your invitation to Diana. Diana, thank Roger for his kind invitation.

DIANA. *(rising, with a touch of exasperation)* Gentlemen, gentlemen! Do be quiet. The fact is *I* planned this party and you're both my guests. So do your telephoning, Roger, and hurry back.

ROGER. You're an angel, Diana. Tea with rum in it, Uncle Edward.

DIANA. Come here, you poor, poor boy.

(She looks gravely into his eyes and gives him a kiss.)

ROGER. *(laughing)* Why am I a poor, poor boy?

DIANA. Well, you are.

(She gives him a light push and he goes out laughing.)

BLAKE. We must act quickly now. I've arranged for some things to happen during this hour. You're going to spill some tea on your dress – no, some chocolate from a chocolate éclair.

DIANA. What?!

BLAKE. And you'll have to go to the ladies' room to clean it up. And you're going to need fifty cents. Open your purse. Give me all the change you have – under a five dollar bill.

DIANA. Why?

BLAKE. Because you'll have to borrow the fifty-cent piece from *him*. – Give me your change.

DIANA. Uncle Edward, you're a devil.

(but she opens her handbag and purse)

BLAKE. *(counting under his breath)* Three quarters. Fifty-cent piece. Dimes. No dollar bills.

DIANA. *(crossing the room, in distress)* Uncle, I don't believe in putting people to tests.

BLAKE. Simply a demonstration –

DIANA. I don't need a demonstration. I suffer enough as it is.

BLAKE. But have you forgotten: we're trying to learn something. Is it a sickness or is it a –

DIANA. Don't say it!

BLAKE. And I want you to notice something else: every subject that comes up in conversation... *(He starts laughing.)*

DIANA. *(suspicious and annoyed)* What?

BLAKE. To call your attention to it, I'll *(He drops his purse.)* drop something. Every subject that comes up in the conversation will have some sort of connection with money.

DIANA. *(angrily drops her handbag)* But that's all you and I have been talking about – until I'm about to go crazy.

BLAKE. Yes...yes, it's contagious.

DIANA. *(with weight)* Uncle Edward, are you trying to break up my engagement?

BLAKE. *(with equal sincerity, but quietly)* No! I'm trying to ratify it...to *save* it.

DIANA. How?

BLAKE. *(emphatic whisper)* With...understanding.

(Enter **PAUL.** *)*

Oh, there you are, Paul. Tea for three and a decanter of rum. And a chocolate éclair for Miss Colvin.

DIANA. But I hate chocolate éclairs!

*(***BLAKE*** looks at her rebukingly.)*

Oh, all right.

BLAKE. And, Paul, when we've finished tea, you'll place the check beside Mr. Osterman.

*(***DIANA*** purposefully drops her lipstick.)*

PAUL. *(picking up the lipstick)* Yes, sir.

DIANA. Thank you, Paul.

*(***PAUL*** goes out.* **DIANA** *leans toward* **BLAKE** *and says confidentially:)*

Now you must play fair. If you cheat, I'll stop the whole thing.

(Enter **ROGER.** *)*

ROGER. All is settled. It's really very exciting. Mother and I setting up a fund where there's a particular particular need.

DIANA. What is it, Roger?

ROGER. *(laughs; then)* Guess where Mother and I are going tomorrow?

DIANA. Where?

ROGER. To the poorhouse!

(BLAKE pushes and drops the ashtray from the table.)

DIANA. *(covering her ears)* Uncle Edward, do be careful!

ROGER. In fact, we're going to three. Mother's already been to thirty – in England and France and Austria – I've been to ten. We're doing something about them. We're making them attractive. Lots of people come to the ends of their lives without pensions, without social security. We're taking the curse off destitution.

BLAKE. And you're taking the curse off superfluity.

(DIANA looks at BLAKE hard and drops her gloves.)

ROGER. We're beginning in a small way. Mother's giving two million and Uncle Henry and I are each giving one. We're not building new homes yet – we're improving the conditions of those that are there. Everywhere we go we ask a thousand questions of superintendents, and of the old men and women…And do you know what these elderly people want most?

(He looks at them expectantly.)

DIANA. *(dropping a shoe)* Money.

ROGER. *(admiringly)* How did you know?!

(DIANA shrugs her shoulders.)

You see, in a sense, they have everything – shelter, clothes, food, companionship. We've scarcely found one who wishes to leave the institution. But they all want the one thing for which there is no provision.

(**PAUL** *enters with a tray – tea; rum; éclair; the service check, which he places on the table beside* **ROGER**; *and a letter.*)

PAUL. A letter has come for you, Mr. Osterman, by special messenger. Will you sign for it, Mr. Osterman?

ROGER. For me? But no one else knows that I'm here.

BLAKE. By special messenger, Paul?

PAUL. Yes, Mr. Blake.

BLAKE. And is the messenger waiting? *(intimately)* Roger… the messenger's waiting in the hall…

ROGER. What?

BLAKE. Fifty cents…for the messenger.

ROGER. *(a study)* But I don't think this is for me.

(He looks at it.)

DIANA. *(taking it from him)* "Roger Osterman, Georgian Room, etc." Yes, I think it's for you.

(**ROGER** *makes some vague gestures toward his pockets.*)

ROGER. Uncle Edward…lend me a quarter, will you?

BLAKE. *(slowly searching his pockets)* A quarter…twenty-five cents…Haven't got it.

ROGER. Paul, give the boy a quarter, will you?

PAUL. *(deaf as a post)* Hot water? Yes, Mr. Osterman –

ROGER. *(loud)* No…a QUARTER, Paul…give the boy a quarter…

PAUL. It's right here, Mr. Osterman.

ROGER. *(has torn the letter open; to* **BLAKE***)* It's from you. You say you'll be here. Well, if the messenger boy is from your own office, you can give him a quarter.

BLAKE. *(smiting his forehead; gives quarter to* **PAUL***)* That's right…Paul…I'll see you…

ROGER. *(dabbing his forehead with his handkerchief)* My, it's hot in here.

DIANA. Roger – you were saying that these old people wanted money. They have everything provided, but they still want money.

ROGER. Yes, I suppose it's to give presents to their nephews and nieces...to one another...They have everything except that...

(He starts laughing; then leans forward confidentially and says:) You know, I think one of the reasons Mother became so interested in all this was...

(Then he stops, laughs again, and says:) Anyway, she's interested.

DIANA. What were you going to say?

ROGER. *(reluctantly)* Well...she's always had the same kind of trouble.

(The other two stare at him.)

Do you know that Mother once pawned a diamond ring?

BLAKE. Your mother went to a pawnshop?

ROGER. No. She sent her maid. Even today she doesn't know that I know. – I was at boarding school, and I'd begun a collection of autographs. More than anything in the world I wanted for my birthday a certain letter of Abraham Lincoln that had come on the market. I couldn't sleep nights I wanted it so bad. But Father thought it was unsuitable that a fifteen year old should get so worked up about a thing like that. – So Mother pawned her ring.

*(**DIANA** rises and crosses the room. She is flushed and serious.)*

DIANA. I don't think we should be talking about such things – but – let me ask one thing, Roger. Your mother has always had a great deal of money of her own?

ROGER. *(laughing)* Yes. But, of course, Father keeps it for her. More than that he's doubled and tripled it.

BLAKE. Of course. It passes through his hands.

ROGER. Yes.

BLAKE. *(looking at **DIANA**)* He sees all the checks. Like the old people in the poorhouse, your mother has everything except money?

ROGER. *(laughing)* Exactly! – The other thing the old people are interested in is food –

DIANA. *(looking down at her dress)* Oh! I've spilled some of that tea and rum on my dress. I must go to the ladies' room and have the spot taken out. Uncle Edward, lend me half a dollar for the attendant.

BLAKE. *(ransacking his pockets)* Half a dollar! Half a dollar! – I told you I hadn't a cent.

ROGER. In institutions – like prisons and poorhouses – you never have any choice –

DIANA. Roger, lend me half a dollar.

ROGER. *(taking out his purse, as he talks)* That was the awful part about prep school – all the food –

*(He hands **DIANA** a ten-dollar bill and goes on talking.)*

– was, so to speak, assigned to you. You never had the least voice in what it would be.

DIANA. But I don't want ten dollars. I want fifty cents.

ROGER. What for?

DIANA. To give the attendant in the ladies' room.

ROGER. Fifty cents? *(rising and inspecting her dress)* I don't see any stain. *(to **BLAKE**)* Borrow it from Paul.

BLAKE. Paul's deaf. Roger, put your hands in your pockets and see if you haven't got fifty cents.

DIANA. *(almost hysterically)* It's all right. The stain's gone away. Forget it, please. Forgive me. I've made a lot of fuss about nothing.

ROGER. *(again touching his forehead with his handkerchief)* Awfully warm in here. We ought to have gone to the club. These places are getting to be regular traps. Why did we come here?

DIANA. What do you mean – traps?

ROGER. You're interrupted all the time – these tiresome demands on you. I love to give, but I don't like to be held up *(gesture of putting a revolver to someone's head)* held up every minute. *(a touch of too much excitement)* I'd like to give everything I've got. I don't care how I live; but I don't like to be forced to give anything. It's not *my* fault that I have money.

DIANA. You're right, Roger.

*(She sees **PAUL**'s service check on the table. She flicks it with her finger and it falls on the floor as near the center of the stage as possible.)*

I don't think of a tip as an expression of thanks. It's just a transaction – a mechanical business convention. Take our waiter, Paul. My thanks is in my smile, so to speak. The money on the table has nothing to do with it.

ROGER. Well, whatever it is, it's a mess.

BLAKE. Once upon a time there was a very poor shepherd. It was in Romania, I think.

DIANA. Uncle!

BLAKE. Every morning this shepherd led his sheep out to a field where there was a great big oak tree.

DIANA. Really, Uncle!

BLAKE. And one day – under that oak tree – he found a large gold piece. The next day he found another. For weeks, for months, for years – every day – he found another gold piece. He bought more sheep. He bought beautiful embroidered shirts.

*(**DIANA** is suddenly overcome with uncontrollable hysterical laughing. She crosses the room, her handkerchief to her mouth, and sits on the bench by the windows. **BLAKE** waits a moment until she has controlled herself.)*

No one else in the village seemed to be finding any gold pieces.

*(**DIANA** sputters a moment. **BLAKE** lowers his voice mysteriously.)*

BLAKE. The shepherd's problem was — *Where do they come from?* And *why* are they given to *him?* Are they, maybe… supernatural?

ROGER. *(sharply)* What?

(**BLAKE** *points to the ceiling.*)

I don't understand a word of this. Uncle Edward, do get on with it. I've never been able to understand these…allegories.

BLAKE. But why to *him?* Was he more intelligent — or more virtuous than the other young men? *(pause)* Now when you find a gold piece every morning, you get used to it. You get to need them. And you are constantly haunted by the fear that the gold pieces will no longer appear under the oak tree. What — oh, what can he do to insure that those blessed gold pieces will continue to arrive every morning?

(**BLAKE**'s *voice turns slightly calculatedly superstitious; he half closes his eyes, shrewdly. His blade-like hand descries an either-or decision or bargain.*)

Obviously, he'd better *give.* In return, so to speak. He gave his town a fine hospital. He gave a beautiful altar to the church.

(He changes his voice to the simple and direct.)

Of course, he gave. But this shepherd was a fine human being, and it was the other question that troubled him most-frightened him, I mean: Why have I been *chosen?*

DIANA. *(sober; her eyes on the floor)* I see that he became frightened.

ROGER. *(looking at* **DIANA**, *in surprise — laughing)* You understand what he's talking about?

DIANA. Frightened, because…if the gold pieces stopped coming, he'd not only be poor…he'd be much more than poor. He'd be exposed. He'd be the man who was formerly fortunate, formerly — what did you say? — intelligent, formerly virtuous and —

BLAKE. *(pointing to the ceiling)* Formerly favored, loved.

DIANA. Far worse than poor.

BLAKE. So he was in the terrible situation of having to GIVE all the time and of having to SAVE all the time.

DIANA. Yes…Yes. – Roger, I have to go. *(She rises.)* Now, who's going to pay the bill? – Roger, you do it, just to show that you like to.

ROGER. *(with charming spontaneity)* Of course, I will. Where is it?

DIANA. *(pointing)* Right there on the floor.

ROGER. *(picking it up)* I'll sign for it. – Where's Paul? There he is!

DIANA. *(putting on lipstick and watching him in her mirror)* Surely, it's not large enough to sign for. There's something small about signing for a three or four dollar charge.

ROGER. *(looking from one to the other)* I don't think so.

BLAKE. Diana's right.

ROGER. *(taking a ten-dollar bill from his purse and laying it on the bill)* Diana, some day you must explain to me slowly what Uncle Edward's been talking about.

*(Enter **PAUL**. **ROGER** indicates the money with his head. **PAUL** makes change quickly.)*

Paul, we're leaving. *(to **DIANA**)* And you must make your Uncle Edward promise not to get tied up in any long rambling stories he can't get out of.

DIANA. *(to **PAUL**)* Thank you, Paul.

BLAKE. Thank you, Paul.

ROGER. Thank you, very much, Paul.

PAUL. *(as he goes out, leaving the bill and change on the table)* You're very welcome.

ROGER. *(While he talks, is feverishly figuring out his change.)* Because I must be very stupid…I can't…

(His hand among the coins of change, he turns and says:)
Because I must say there are lots of better things to talk about than what we've been…

(He stops while he studies the change before him.)

ROGER. In fact, in our family we make it a rule never to talk about money at all... *(pause)* I don't think you realize, Diana, that my life is enough of a hell as it is: the only way I can cope with it is to never talk about it...what am I doing here?...

DIANA. *(going toward him; soothingly)* What's the matter, dear? Just leave him a quarter.

ROGER. *(His face lighting up.)* Would that be all right?

(She nods.)

Diana, you're an angel. *(triumphantly)* I'm going to leave him fifty cents, just to show him I love you.

DIANA. No. I'm not an angel. I'm a very human being. I'll need to be fed. And clothed. And –

ROGER. *(bewitched; kissing her gravely)* I'll see you have everything.

DIANA. I can look forward to everything?

ROGER. Yes.

DIANA. Like those old ladies in the poorhouse, I can look forward to –

ROGER. My giving you everything.

*(**DIANA** hurries out ever so lightly, blowing her nose. **PAUL** appears at the door. **BLAKE** and **ROGER** go out. **PAUL**, alone, picks up the tip. No expression on his face. **DIANA** appears quickly.)*

DIANA. I dropped a glove.

(She drops a dollar bill on the table.)

Goodbye, Paul.

PAUL. Goodbye, Miss Colvin.

(They go out.)

End of Play

THORNTON WILDER (1897-1975) was an accomplished novelist and playwright whose works explore the connection between the commonplace and the cosmic dimensions of human experience. He won three Pulitzer Prizes: for his novel *The Bridge of San Luis Rey*, and two plays, *Our Town* and *The Skin of Our Teeth*. Wilder's farce, *The Matchmaker*, was adapted as the musical *Hello, Dolly!* He also enjoyed enormous success as a translator, adaptor, actor, librettist and lecturer/teacher. Wilder's many honors include the Gold Medal for Fiction from the American Academy of Arts and Letters and the Presidential Medal of Freedom. Penelope Niven's definitive biography, *Thornton Wilder: A Life*, was published in October 2012. For more information, please visit www.thorntonwilder.com.

Also by
Thornton Wilder...

The Alcestiad

The Beaux' Stratagem (with Ken Ludwig)

The Matchmaker

Our Town

The Skin of Our Teeth

<u>Thornton Wilder One Act Series: The Ages of Man</u>

Infancy

Childhood

Youth

The Rivers Under the Earth

<u>Thornton Wilder One Act Series: Wilder's Classic One Acts</u>

The Long Christmas Dinner

Queens of France

Pullman Car Hiawatha

Love and How to Cure It

Such Things Only Happen in Books

The Happy Journey to Trenton and Camden

<u>Thornton Wilder One Act Series: The Seven Deadly Sins</u>

The Drunken Sisters

Bernice

The Wreck on the 5:25

A Ringing of Doorbells

In Shakespeare and the Bible

Someone From Assisi

Cement Hands

Please visit our website **samuelfrench.com** for complete descriptions and licensing information.

www.ingramcontent.com/pod-product-compliance
Lightning Source LLC
Chambersburg PA
CBHW071847290426
44109CB00017B/1962